Are unicorn...?

Contents

Written by Isabel Thomas

Collins

1 Have you seen a unicorn?

Your answer is probably yes – and no!

Most people have seen *pictures* of unicorns. We know what unicorns look like.

Let's prove it! Can you spot the unicorn on these pages?

2

Most people know that unicorns have:

- four legs, like a horse
- white fur, like a polar bear
- one horn, like a rhino.

But there is a big difference between unicorns and these other animals.

No one has ever seen a unicorn in real life. We can't spot unicorns on a farm, visit them at a zoo or see them on safari. There are no photographs of unicorns in the wild.

Does this mean that unicorns aren't real?

After all, there are lots of other animals that can't be seen on farms, at zoos, or in the wild.

No one has ever seen a dinosaur in real life. There are no photographs of dinosaurs. Just like unicorns, we only see dinosaurs in stories, films and drawings. But we know that dinosaurs *were* real animals that stomped around planet Earth millions of years ago.

Could unicorns also be ancient animals that became **extinct**, like the dinosaurs? Or do they only exist in our imaginations?

To find out, we need to go back in time and look at the very first stories about unicorns. How did these stories begin? Is there any **evidence** that unicorns once existed? Is there any evidence that they still do?

2 The first unicorns

Two thousand years ago, most people thought that unicorns were real. We know this because of the things written in ancient books.

One of the oldest books that mentions unicorns was written by a doctor called Ctesias in Ancient Greece.

This doctor travelled a lot and ended up working for the King of Persia – a country that is now called Iran. He heard about amazing animals that lived in nearby India.

There were no cameras then, but the doctor knew people in Greece would love to hear about these animals too.

He wrote a book describing ...

talking birds ...

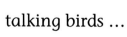

super-strong elephants …

human-eating cats …

and a donkey with one horn:

"In India there are wild asses as large as horses, or even larger. Their body is white, their head dark red, their eyes bluish, and they have a horn in their forehead."

To people in Ancient Greece, these animals sounded very strange. At first, they laughed at the idea of talking birds and human-eating cats!

But over time, they learnt that parrots, tigers and elephants were real animals, and that parrots really can mimic human words!

Could one-horned donkeys be real too?

The Greek doctor had described them in lots of detail. He even said he had held a bone from one of these donkeys in his hands.

swift and strong

fierce fighter

one and a half cubits long

red head

deep blue eyes

white and black horn with a red tip

white body

A cubit is an old measurement. It is about 45 centimetres, roughly as long as a grown-up's **forearm**. FACT

9

Soon, other people were including one-horned donkeys and horses in their own books about real animals! This timeline shows some of the most famous.

350 BCE: An Ancient Greek scientist called Aristotle wrote a *History of Animals*. He included an Indian donkey with one horn.

c200 CE: A Roman author and teacher called Aelian wrote about unicorns in his book *On the Nature of Animals*. He said they had a red mane and a sharp, spiralling horn.

77 CE: In *Natural History*, a Roman author called Pliny described a monoceros. It had a body like a horse, a head like a deer, feet like an elephant, and one long, black horn.

The name monoceros came from the Greek words *monos* (one) and *keras* (horn). Roman writers translated this into their own language. In Latin, *unus* means one and *cornu* means horn. This gave us the word unicorn.

FACT

c545 CE: A Greek traveller called Cosmas drew tiny pictures of animals he saw on his travels in Asia. One of them was a unicorn! He wrote that its horn gave it special powers, helping it to land after a fall.

1470s: The Italian artist, Leonardo da Vinci drew a unicorn in his notebook.

1200s: The famous explorer Marco Polo said he had seen unicorns on his travels.

For hundreds of years, books and drawings were the only way to learn about animals in faraway places. So, people thought unicorns were just as real as elephants or tigers!

You might think it sounds strange to believe something you have only read about. But we still do this today.

Can you think of any animals you have only seen in books?

How do you know they *really* exist?

Because there are pictures? Because a grown-up says so? Because an expert wrote the book?

Today, fake animal news can spread quickly.
During the coronavirus pandemic, someone made up
a story that lions had been released in Russian cities
to make people stay at home! The fake news
spread quickly. It even had photos.

Scientists have a rule to tell if something is real.
They ask for **empirical evidence**. This means seeing
something with your own eyes instead of just believing
what you are told.

Is there any empirical evidence for unicorns?

3 Unicorn horns

In the 15th and 16th centuries, people thought they had found empirical evidence that unicorns were real.

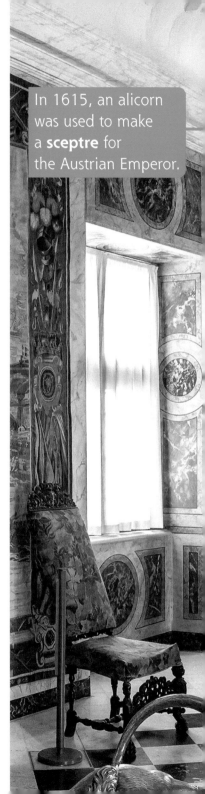

In 1615, an alicorn was used to make a **sceptre** for the Austrian Emperor.

People began buying and selling "unicorn horns". They were known as **alicorns**.

At first, alicorns were very expensive. They were worth 20 times more than gold! Only very rich people could afford them. It was like owning an expensive sports car today!

In 1468, alicorns were used as special decorations at a royal wedding.

In the 16th century, Queen Elizabeth I was given "the horn of a unicorn" as a gift. It became known as the Horn of Windsor.

In 1584, the **Tsar** of Russia held an alicorn while he was crowned.

In 1671, the Throne Chair of Denmark was made using alicorns!

Ordinary people couldn't afford a whole alicorn, but they could buy small pieces of alicorn or alicorn powder. This was popular because unicorn horns were thought to have special powers, like protecting people from poisons, or healing illnesses.

Where did this idea come from?

Do you remember the Ancient Greek doctor who first wrote about unicorns? He mentioned their special powers too. He probably got the idea from even older books from Ancient China, where people used animal horns to detect poisons or as medicine.

For hundreds of years, this rumour was passed on.

In one famous book, Hildegard of Bingen wrote that unicorns could cure **dreaded** diseases.

Today, most people know that animal horns don't have special powers. They are made from the same stuff as our hair! But some people still believe fake stories that powdered rhino horn can cure illnesses. So many rhinos are killed for their horns, they are in danger of becoming extinct.

FACT

We can see photos of objects made from alicorn. We can even visit these objects in museums! Is this evidence that unicorns are real?

The long, twisted alicorns themselves are real. We can see them with our eyes and hold them in our hands. But today, we know that they belonged to a totally different animal.

There are clues in the way people described alicorns.

But when explorers and sailors from Europe first saw narwhals in the 13th century, they were amazed. They mistook narwhals for unicorns!

People began to hunt the narwhals and collect their tusks. Back in Europe, they could be sold for lots of money.

Many people believed that the tusks were alicorns (unicorn horns). They began painting pictures of unicorns with long, spiralling horns, just like a narwhal's tusk!

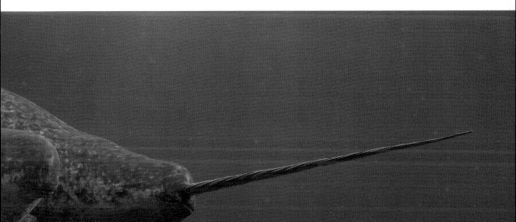

But not everyone believed alicorns – or unicorns – were real.

In 1638, a scientist called Ole Worm found a tusk that was still attached to the skull of a narwhal. This proved that alicorns were from whales, not horses.

The word spread. But people kept on buying and selling alicorn for another hundred years. Just 300 years ago, doctors were still giving people alicorn as medicine!

Most alicorn was fake. It didn't come from a unicorn or even a narwhal, but from powdered animal bones, **fossils**, or **stalactites**!

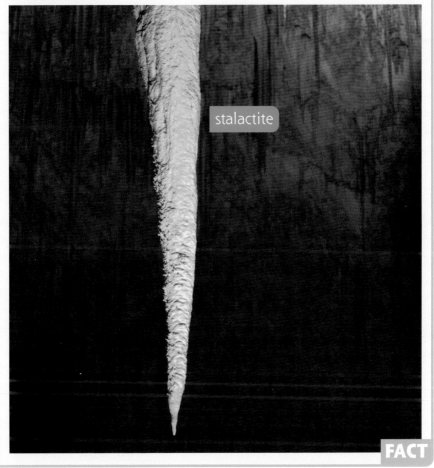

stalactite

FACT

Narwhals and their tusks helped unicorn stories and rumours survive. But how did they get started in the first place? Are there any land animals that might have been mistaken for unicorns?

4 Real "unicorns"

The narwhal helped to shape ideas about what unicorn horns looked like. But unicorns were already famous before narwhal tusks were discovered.

The first stories might be based on different beasts – real animals that lived on land! Which beasts might these be? We can find clues in the very first unicorn stories. They all came from the same part of the world – the high mountains of northern India, Nepal and the Chinese region of Tibet.

Two thousand years ago, they were home to lots of amazing animals. But because the mountains are so hard to travel through, few people got to see these animals with their own eyes. They had to rely on stories, passed from person to person.

24

The Himalayas

Some people think that the first unicorn stories were based on these real-life animals. What do you think?

Indian rhinoceros
The Indian rhinoceros has one horn. But the horn is on the tip of its nose, not its forehead.
Some people said that unicorns had feet like elephants.

Indian antelope / Blackbuck
Indian antelopes live in India and Nepal. Their horns look like corkscrews.

Onager / Wild ass / Kiang
Wild horses were common 2,000 years ago. They were fierce and fast. But they didn't have horns!

Wild yak
Wild yaks are huge cattle that live in the Himalayas. They have large white horns.

Tibetan antelope / Chiru
These mountain goats have hooves and beautiful long black horns. Many early stories about unicorns said they had black horns.

Other people think the first unicorn stories might have been based on a mistake!

When the Greek doctor Ctesias was working for the King of Persia, he probably saw pictures like this:

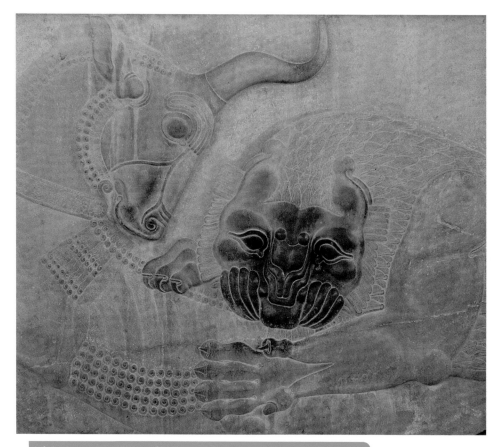

This is a carving of a lion biting a horned animal.
The animal seems to have just one horn.
But perhaps the artist was trying to show
a two-horned animal from the side!

From the side, this Himalayan oryx looks like it has just one horn.

These links to real animals and real art would have made unicorn stories more believable! Especially when people began selling narwhal tusks.

As time went on, people realised the tusks belonged to narwhals. The only one-horned animals they came across in real life were rhinos.

Why were unicorns still so popular? To answer this, we need to find out what people think of when they think about unicorns.

5 Unicorns as symbols

What kind of animal do you think a unicorn is?
Many people pick words like:

noble

brave

fierce

courageous

bold

kind

good

Two thousand years ago, the Greek doctor Ctesias described unicorns that were fast, strong and would fight to the death to protect their young.

Since then, unicorns have become **symbols** of good qualities.

In Ancient Persia, spotting an Indian rhino or karkadann was thought to bring good luck.
This may have led to the unicorn becoming a symbol of good luck.

In the Middle Ages, unicorns became very important symbols. At first, they were said to be small and shy, but **invincible**.

Lots of artists used unicorns in their ...

tapestries

stone carvings

paintings

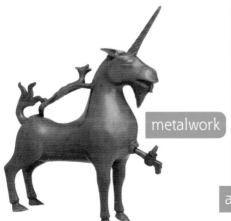

metalwork

and books.

31

Unicorns also became a symbol of love.

This explains why Margaret of York and Charles the Bold had unicorn horn decorations at their wedding in 1468!

This was also the time when people began selling the tusks of narwhals, pretending they were unicorn horns. Artists began to imagine bigger unicorns with pure white coats, and long, spiralling horns.

Soon, people were imagining unicorns as the strongest animals of all! They became a symbol of strength and power.

Unicorns were used on **coats of arms**. Over time, unicorns became the national animal of Scotland.

In the 12th century, the King of Scotland added a unicorn to the Scottish coat of arms.

In the 17th century, the Scottish Royal coat of arms had two unicorns holding a shield.

The unicorn also appears on the Royal coat of arms of the United Kingdom. You can spot this coat of arms on coins and banknotes, in courtrooms and on passports.

Once you start looking, you will find unicorns hidden everywhere!

In the early 19th century, unicorns were still very popular. But fewer people believed they were real animals. Every time someone found evidence of unicorns, it turned out to be fake!

The fake unicorn

In 1663, miners came across some ancient bones in a cave in Germany. Otto von Guericke heard about the discovery. He put the bones together like this:

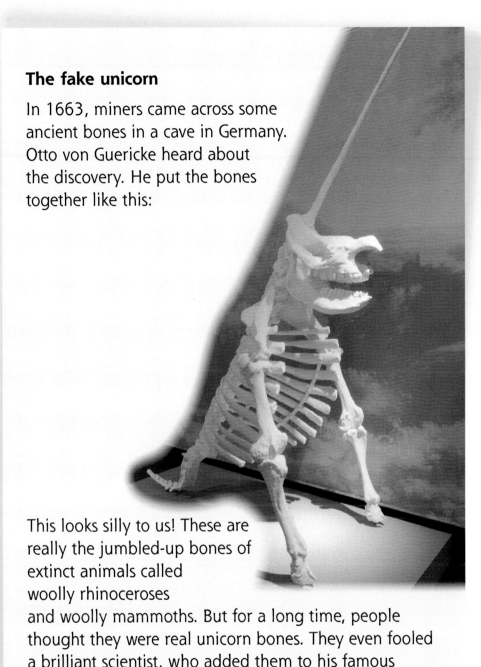

This looks silly to us! These are really the jumbled-up bones of extinct animals called woolly rhinoceroses and woolly mammoths. But for a long time, people thought they were real unicorn bones. They even fooled a brilliant scientist, who added them to his famous science book. This shows how easily fake news can spread!

6 Looking for unicorns

Some people still wanted to believe that unicorns were real. By the 19th century, it was much easier for people to travel to other parts of the world. Some explorers set out to look for real-life unicorns.

At first, they travelled to central Asia, where the very first unicorn stories began.

Then, people in Europe began to hear about the amazing animals of Africa – such as striped zebras and tall giraffes. They wondered if the huge forests of central Africa were also home to unicorns.

The people of central Africa knew lots about local animals. They told explorers about a strange, colourful animal called an atti. It was about the size of a horse but more like a giraffe, and the males had horns. Could this be the unicorn, at last?

Turn the page to find out …

The mysterious atti turned out to be one of the most amazing mammals ever!

blue tongue

striped coat

horns

But it was not a unicorn! Today we call it an okapi.

Two thousand years after they were first described, no one has ever found evidence of a real unicorn.

We've found fossils of hundreds of different dinosaurs, but no one has ever found a unicorn fossil.

Fossils form when traces of a plant or animal become **preserved** in rock. If we find a fossil, we know that creature must have once lived on Earth. By measuring how old the rock is, we can work out when!

We have found fossils of ancient rhinos. This one is known as the Siberian unicorn.

FACT

By the end of the 19th century, most people had stopped believing that unicorns were real animals.

But unicorns as symbols of strength and power were more popular than ever!

HMS *Unicorn* is a Royal Navy ship, first launched in 1824. It is one of the six remaining oldest ships in the world.

In the 19th century, unicorns also became popular characters in stories. They were often brave, gentle and kind. Sometimes they had magical powers.

In 1812, the Brothers Grimm included a unicorn in a fairy tale.

"Well, now that we have seen each other,"
said the unicorn, "if you'll believe in me,
I'll believe in you."
– *Through the Looking-Glass*, Lewis Carroll, 1871

Unicorn books, films
and toys are still
very popular today.

7 Are unicorns real?

The first unicorn stories were probably written by people who had never seen a unicorn in real life. They might have heard stories or seen art of animals with just one horn.

For 2,000 years, many people believed these stories. They thought unicorns were real.

Then science taught that the best way to find out about the world is to look for evidence, instead of just accepting what we are told.

No one has found any evidence that unicorns are real animals. But stories of unicorns were probably based on real animals – like rhinos, antelopes, narwhals and okapis. These animals are just as amazing as unicorns!

Today, we know that unicorns are probably not real. But lots of books and films still feature unicorns. They are symbols of bravery, kindness and hope!

No wonder people want to believe in unicorns!

Glossary

alicorns an old name for unicorn horns, and for the material it was thought to be made of

coats of arms special pictures that represent a person, family, or country; they often combine lots of symbols together

dreaded really feared

empirical evidence information that we have seen, heard, felt, smelt or tasted ourselves

evidence facts or information that can tell us if a belief or idea is true or correct

extinct used to be alive, but no longer exists

forearm the part of a person's arm from the elbow to the hand

fossils rocks that take the shape of the remains of a living thing

invincible too strong to be defeated

preserved when something is protected or made to last

sceptre a long staff or stick, decorated and carried by rulers as a symbol of their power

stalactites long, pointed structures that form in a cave, as water drips from the roof of the cave. As the water evaporates, it leaves behind the minerals dissolved in it.

symbols things that have an extra meaning or meanings; things that stand for something else

Tsar an old name for a ruler of Russia (pronounced 'Zar')

Index

Unicorns around the world

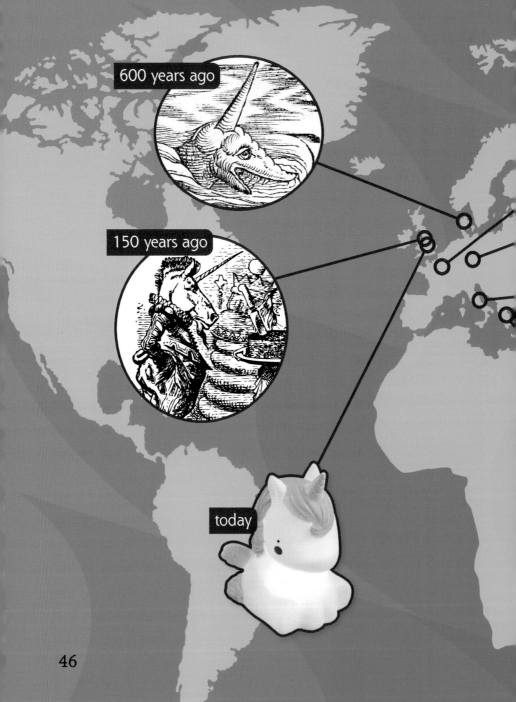

600 years ago

150 years ago

today

500 years ago

350 years ago

1,950 years ago

800 years ago

2,300 years ago

2,500 years ago

47

Ideas for reading

Written by Christine Whitney
Primary Literacy Consultant

Reading objectives:
- be introduced to non-fiction books that are structured in different ways
- listen to, discuss and express views about non-fiction
- retrieve and record information from non-fiction
- discuss and clarify the meanings of words

Spoken language objectives:
- participate in discussion
- speculate, hypothesise, imagine and explore ideas through talk
- ask relevant questions

Curriculum links: Science: Explore the differences between things that are living, dead, and things that have never been alive; Writing: Write for different purposes

Word count: 3142

Interest words: extinct, evidence, symbols

Resources: Paper, pencils and crayons, access to the internet.

Build a context for reading

- Ask children if they have ever seen a unicorn in real life. Can they describe a unicorn to their partner?
- Now turn to the book and read the blurb on the back cover. Ask children if they believe that unicorns were *ancient animals that became extinct, like the dinosaurs.*
- Introduce the word *evidence*. Ask children to explain what this word means and to suggest a sentence which uses this word correctly.

Understand and apply reading strategies

- Turn to the contents page and read through the different sections in the book. Ask for volunteers to say which section they are most interested in reading and why.
- Read together pages 2–9. Ask children to explain why people thought that unicorns were real.
- On page 21, it says that people *mistook narwhals for unicorns.* Ask children to explain why this was so.